LOG HORIZON
THE WEST WIND BRIGADE

[CONTENTS]

LOG HORIZON **THE WEST WIND BRIGADE** 10

LOG HORIZON
THE WEST WIND BRIGADE

GOUN (RUMM)
GOUN
GOUN
CHAPTER: 54 Will
(WAKE)

GOUN (RUMM)
ゴゥン
......
GOUN
ゴゥン

WHAT'S ...
...GOING ON?

WHAT HAP-PENED?
GOUN
ゴゥン
I CAN'T REALLY REMEMB-BER.
GOUN
ゴゥン

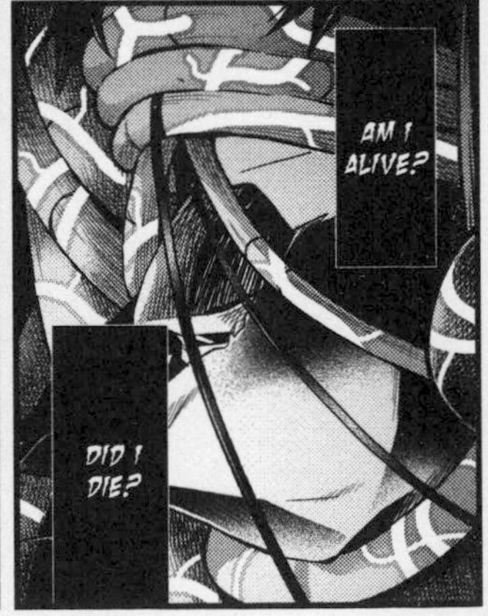
AM I ALIVE?
DID I DIE?

THE ONLY THING THAT'S CLEAR...
GU (STRAIN) GU

...IS THE
VAST
AMOUNT
OF
MANA...
...THAT'S
FLOWING
INTO MY
BODY.
ZU
(ZZZT)
ZU

THAT'S
RIGHT—
THIS MAGIC
POWER IS
WHAT LED ME
HERE.

POTA
(DRIP)
POTA

GOUN
(RUMM)
GOUN

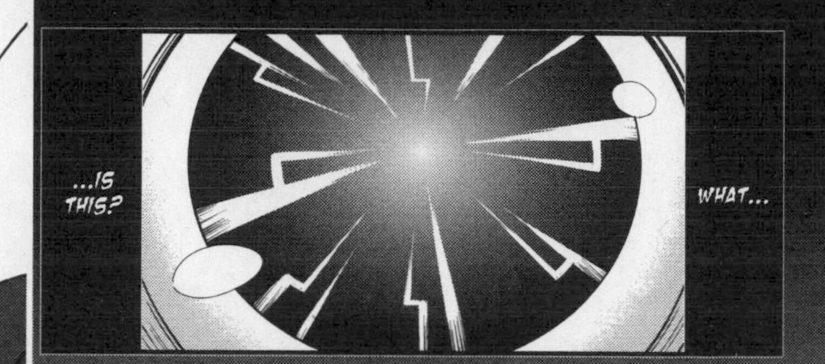
WHAT...
...IS THIS?

—NOW I KNOW.

I CAN FEEL THE POWER'S TRUE NATURE...
...AS IT COURSES THROUGH ME.

IT TAKES AN ENORMOUS AMOUNT OF MANA TO POWER THE GUARDS' MOBILE ARMOR, WHICH CAN TAKE DOWN ADVENTURERS...
...AND TO KEEP THE ANCIENT DEVICE THAT GENERATES A BARRIER OVER THE ENTIRE TOWN, TO PREVENT MONSTER INVASIONS, CONTINUOUSLY OPERATING.
IN ORDER TO SUPPLY ALL OF THAT ENERGY...
...THEY BUILT A GIGANTIC MAGIC CIRCLE UNDER THE WHOLE TOWN.

THIS POWER...

...IS AKIBA ITSELF.

DOKUN
(BADMP)
DOKUN

KUROE?

HE'S COMING ...

HE'LL BE HERE AGAIN...
...REALLY SOON...

CAN YOU TELL WHERE THE EQUIPMENT HUNTER IS?
...NOT CLEARLY.

BUT I CAN FEEL HIM.
HIS PRESENCE IS GETTING STRONGER.

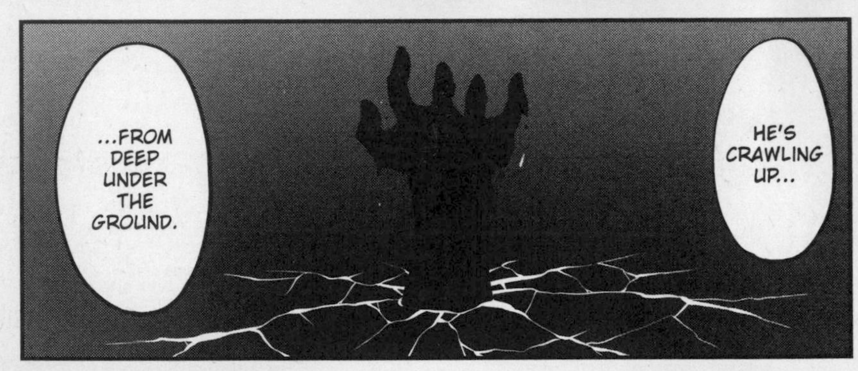
HE'S CRAWLING UP...
...FROM DEEP UNDER THE GROUND.

WE'RE PULLED TO EACH OTHER...
I CAN'T GET AWAY...

SU (SHUF)

GYU (SQUEEZE)

IT'S ALL RIGHT ...
YOU'LL BE OKAY.

......

SAY, KUROE? CAN I ASK YOU SOME-THING?

CAN'T YOU FIGHT THE WAY THE EQUIPMENT HUNTER DOES?

I MEAN...
...I'M NOT SAYING YOU SHOULD FIGHT TOO...

THE STRENGTH TO FIGHT...?
IT'S JUST, IF YOU HAD THE STRENGTH FOR THAT, IT WOULD BE EASIER TO PROTECT YOURSELF, Y'KNOW?
IF YOU ABSORBED MANA LIKE THE EQUIPMENT HUNTER DOES...
...YOUR BODY MIGHT GET BIGGER TOO.
...ME?
WITH ALL DUE RESPECT...
!
...I THINK THAT WOULD BE QUITE DIFFICULT.

MAGUS-SAN AND I TOOK OUR SPECULATIONS ABOUT THE EQUIPMENT HUNTER AS FAR AS WE COULD.
ZU (SLURP) ZU

FIRST, LET ME EXPLAIN WHY I BELIEVE KUROE-SAN IS UNABLE TO FIGHT.

THE EQUIPMENT HUNTER AND KUROE-SAN WERE ORIGINALLY ONE BEING.
NOW THAT THE TWO CORES ARE SEPARATE...
...I DON'T THINK IT WOULD BE ODD FOR KUROE-SAN TO HAVE THE SAME CHARACTERISTICS AS THE EQUIPMENT HUNTER.

HOWEVER, I BELIEVE THERE IS A *CRUCIAL DIFFERENCE* BETWEEN THE TWO CORES.
THAT IS— WHEN THEY EXISTED IN THE SAME BODY...
...ONE CORE GOVERNED "YANG ENERGY" ...
...WHILE THE OTHER GOVERNED "YIN ENERGY."
THE EQUIPMENT HUNTER, WHICH TARGETS ADVENTURER EQUIPMENT...
...MOST LIKELY HAS THE YANG ENERGY CORE.
AS YOU KNOW, YANG ENERGY IS THE ENERGY POWERING THE SPIRIT AND MANA.
THE EQUIPMENT HUNTER ABSORBS ENERGY BY EATING HIGH-RARITY ITEMS THAT POSSESS MANA.
ON THE OTHER HAND, KUROE-SAN HAS THE CORE THAT COMPLEMENTS THE EQUIPMENT HUNTER'S.
IT SHOULD GOVERN YIN ENERGY— THE ENERGY OF THE PHYSICAL BODY.

GU (FLEX)
STRONG YIN ENERGY IS DIRECTLY LINKED TO PHYSICAL VIGOR AND A STRONG FIGHTING SPIRIT.

IN OTHER WORDS, FOR KUROE-SAN TO REACH A LEVEL AT WHICH SHE COULD FIGHT...
...SHE'D HAVE TO ABSORB ENERGY FROM DIFFERENT SOURCES THAN THE EQUIPMENT HUNTER.

SUCH AS, FOR EXAMPLE...
...THE PHYSICAL BODIES OF HIGH-LEVEL ADVENTURERS, YOU SEE...

I...I DON'T EAT ADVENTURERS...
YES, WE KNOW THAT.

IT'S NOT ABOUT WHETHER YOU DO OR NOT.
YOU PROBABLY CAN'T.
MEANING...?

IT'S DUE TO THAT OTHER CHARACTERISTIC THE CORES HAVE.

THE KEY TO THE CORES' ABILITIES LIES IN COPYING INFORMATION FROM AN ADVENTURER'S "SPIRIT"... RIGHT?

THE EQUIP HUNTER COPIED SOUJIROU-KUN'S DATA, AND NOW HE HAS HIS SHAPE.

HE'S NOT EXACTLY LIKE YOU, THOUGH. THERE ARE DIFFERENC-ES HERE AND THERE, RIGHT?
HE STILL HAS TRACES OF HIS PRIOR FORM MIXED IN.

THE MIXTURE IS MORE OBVIOUS WITH HIS MENTAL STATE.
HIS THOUGHTS, FEELINGS, AND MEMORIES...
...SEEMED VERY UNSTABLE— AS IF THEY DIDN'T BELONG TO SOUJIROU-KUN OR THE ONE BEFORE HIM.

YOU CAN'T TAKE IN SOMEONE ELSE'S ENTIRE BEING JUST AS IT IS, YOU KNOW?
IT'S GOTTA BE IMPOSSIBLE FOR THE PERSONALITIES HE COPIED TO BLEND NEATLY.

THAT'S WHY THE EQUIP HUNTER AVOIDS INFLICTING DIRECT DAMAGE ON ADVENTURERS.
HE PROBABLY KNOWS THAT IF HE GETS THEIR BLOOD ON HIM AND ACQUIRES MORE UNNECESSARY PERSONALITIES, HE'LL BREAK.
GA (GRAB)
DA (DASH)

THAT BEING THE CASE, IF KUROE-SAN TRIED TO ACQUIRE LARGE AMOUNTS OF YIN ENERGY, THE SOURCE OF HER OWN ENERGY...
...THE VERY ACT OF DOING SO WOULD DAMAGE HER.
I SEE...

BECAUSE THAT'S TRUE, WE CAN DEDUCE ONE MORE THING.

IT'S ABOUT THE ONE WEAPON THAT THE EQUIP HUNTER HESITATED TO EAT—
KOGA-RASU-MARU.

KOGA-RASU-MARU IS FANTASY-CLASS, SUPER-RARE EQUIP-MENT.
ITS ABILITY IS COMBAT SUPPORT FROM THE AVATAR THAT DWELLS IN THE SWORD.

I THINK THE KATANA'S AVATAR IS THE KEY HERE.

IN THE GAME, KOGARASU-MARU PROVIDED COMBAT SUPPORT FOR ITS BEARER AS AN AI...
...BUT NOW, ALTHOUGH THE PEOPLE OF THE EARTH WERE ORIGINALLY AIS, THEY HAVE PERSONALITIES. KOGARASU-MARU MUST BE SIMILAR.

AS A MATTER OF FACT, KOGARASU-MARU HAS DISPLAYED ITS *WILL* ONCE.

ORDINARILY, FANTASY-CLASS ITEMS CAN ONLY BE USED BY THEIR OWNERS.
IN THE GAME, THIS WAS PROBABLY INTENDED ...
...TO PREVENT CASUAL TRANSFERS AND TRADES, AND TO BLOCK "REAL MONEY" TRANSAC-TIONS.
IN TERMS OF THIS WORLD, COULDN'T WE THINK OF IT AS LEGENDARY EQUIPMENT *CHOOSING ITS OWN BEARER*?

JUST ONCE, THOUGH, KOGA-RASU-MARU...
...LET SOMEONE BESIDES SOUJIROU-KUN WIELD IT.

COME TO THINK OF IT...!

...I THINK KOGARASUMARU, WHICH USED TO BE AI EQUIPMENT, HAS A PARTICULARLY STRONG, INDEPENDENT WILL IN THIS WORLD.

I DON'T KNOW WHETHER IT WAS TO SAVE YOU FROM HARM...
...OR WHETHER THE KATANA RECOG-NIZED ITS BEARER'S COMRADE, BUT...

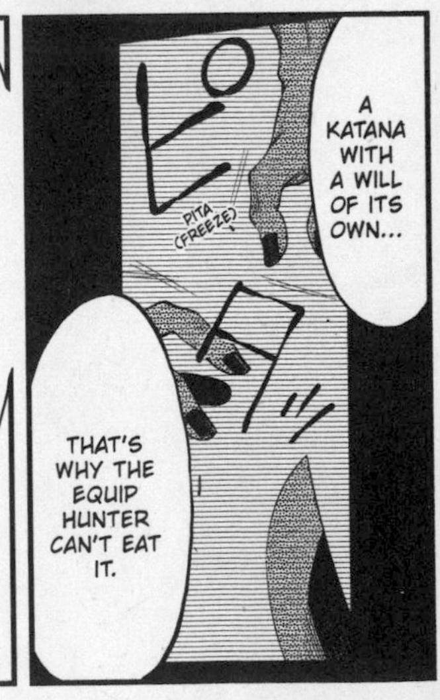
A KATANA WITH A WILL OF ITS OWN...
PITA (FREEZE)
THAT'S WHY THE EQUIP HUNTER CAN'T EAT IT.

IT'S A BIG ADVANTAGE FOR US, SINCE OUR OPPONENT EATS THE WEAPONS THAT ATTACK IT TO BOOST ITS OWN ENERGY.

SOUJIROU-KUN, AS KOGARASU-MARU'S BEARER...
...YOU'RE ONE OF THE EQUIP HUNTER'S FEW NATURAL ENEMIES.

LOG HORIZON
THE WEST WIND BRIGADE

LOG HORIZON
THE WEST WIND BRIGADE

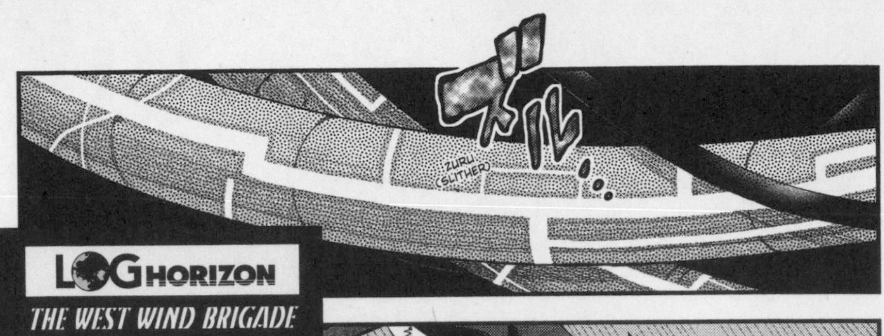

LOG HORIZON

THE WEST WIND BRIGADE

CHAPTER : 55 Preparing for Battle

NAZUNA—HAVE EVERYONE GET READY, SO WE CAN HEAD OUT ANYTIME.

WHAT KIND OF TEAM?
OUR ENEMY IS A HU-MAN-OID...
IF WE'RE A BIG GROUP AND IT TURNS INTO A MELEE, IT'LL BE HARD TO FIGHT.

ONE UNIT TO STRIKE THE EQUIP HUNTER AND ONE TO PROTECT KUROE—
MAKE IT A HALF-RAID SYSTEM OF TWO SIX-PEOPLE UNITS.
GOT IT.

DADDY...

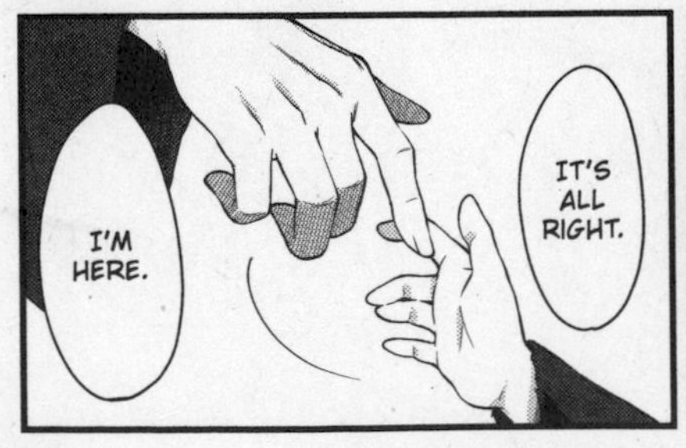
IT'S ALL RIGHT.
I'M HERE.

......
DADDY... BE CAREFUL...
HIS POWER IS...
...MUCH, MUCH STRONGER THAN BEFORE.

NO ONE'S REPORTED DAMAGE FROM THE EQUIP HUNTER IN THE PAST FEW DAYS.
WHERE IS HE GETTING MANA?

ZAAAA (FWIIIIISH)

ZURU (SLITHER)
I COULD JUST CRUSH THEM ALL IN TOWN, ADVENTURERS AND GUARDS ALIKE, BUT...
DO
DO
DO
DO (THUD)
SHURURU (SHLOOLOO)

ZU (SLUCK)
ZU
DOKUN (BADMP)
DOKUN
DON'T BE HASTY...
DOKUN

DOKUN
YOU'RE NOT COMPLETE YET...
DOKUN
TAKE BACK THE CORE FIRST...

DADDY... I...
I HAVE TO GO...

I DON'T WANT TO, BUT I...
I CAN'T FIGHT IT...

I'D REALLY PREFER YOU TO STAY SOMEWHERE SAFE, KUROE...

...BUT I THINK YOU NEED TO FACE THE EQUIP HUNTER...
...AND SEVER YOUR TIES.

SO...
...LET'S GO TOGETHER.

I-I...
I'LL GO TELL NAZUNA-SAN!

SARA-CHAN...

THOSE SEEDS WE PLANTED...
WHEN WILL THEY SPROUT...?
SOON...
ANY DAY NOW.
I SEE...
FU-FU... I CAN'T WAIT...
SAY, DADDY...
THE TOWN...
TREES...
PEO-PLE...
FLOW-ERS...
ORDINARY CONVER-SATIONS...
THE MEALS WE ALL ATE TOGETHER...

IT WASN'T MY FIRST TIME SEEING AND DOING THOSE THINGS.
OR AT LEAST, THEY SHOULDN'T HAVE BEEN FIRSTS TO ME, BUT...

...HERE IT WAS COMPLETELY DIFFERENT.

IT WASN'T THE SAME AS IT WAS IN THE DARK-NESS.
EVERY-THING SHONE SO BRIGHTLY...

DADDY... I...
I WANT TO COME HOME TO THIS PLACE AGAIN.

KURO-CHAN...

... YES.

WE'LL ALL...

...COME BACK HOME TOGETHER.

ZA (FOON)
EVERY-ONE!
ARE YOU READY?
YOU BET I AM!

Y...
YES! WE'RE READY TO GO!!
I'M RARING TO GOOO.
HOW DARE THERE BE A FAKE SOU-SAMA.
A KNOCKOFF VERSION OF MAGGOT-MAN?
IT DOESN'T GET MORE OBNOXIOUS THAN THAT!
LET'S DOOO THIS!
...YES'M.
GLAD TO HEAR IT.
LISTEN ...

YOU'RE PUTTING ME ON THE TEAM?
...ARE YOU NUTS?
MY LEVEL'S NOT THAT HIGH.
BESIDES, THERE MUST BE GUILD MEMBERS YOU COULD TRUST MORE...
HEY, I TRUST YOU.
YOU'RE SMART...
BUT—
... AND...
...YOU KNOW A LOT ABOUT THE EQUIPMENT HUNTER...

...YOU LIKE SOUJI...
...ABOUT AS MUCH AS WE DO.

KAA (BLUSH)
I—
I WAS REALLY AWFUL TO YOU...

NOBODY CARES ANYMORE.

IF YOU THINK YOU'VE DONE US WRONG...
...PAY US BACK IN PHYSICAL LABOR.

YEAH, I KNOW.
THEY SAID TO TELL YOU EVERYBODY'S READY.
I'LL BE RIGHT THERE.
HERE.
HM?
UM...
FORE-HEAD... I MEAN...
... ISAMI ...
... CHAN.

RODERICK... SAN AND I...MADE IT.
I DON'T KNOW IF IT'LL WORK ON THE EQUIP HUNTER OR NOT...
IT WOULD BE BEST IF WE DIDN'T HAVE TO USE IT AT ALL, BUT...

...IF THINGS GET REALLY BAD...
...IT MIGHT BE... USEFUL.
NO GUAR-AN-TEES, BUT...

UH-HUH!
THANKS, MAGUS-CHAN!

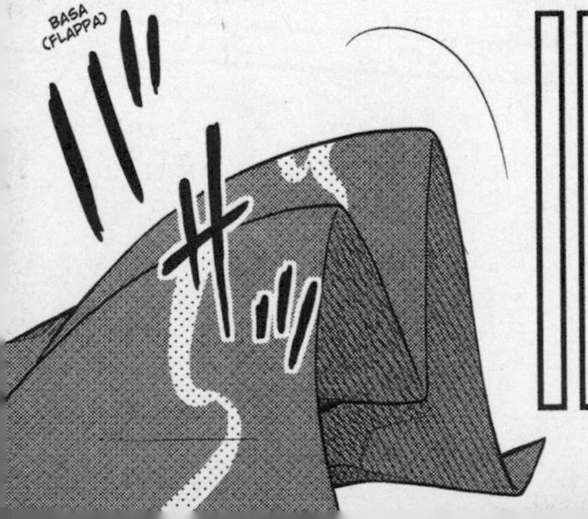
BASA (FLAPPA)

ZA
(TA-DAA)

I THINK KOGARASU-MARU, WHICH USED TO BE AI EQUIPMENT ...
...HAS A PARTICULARLY STRONG, INDEPENDENT WILL IN THIS WORLD.
UP UNTIL NOW...YOU'VE PROTECTED ME INTENTIONALLY, HAVEN'T YOU?

THANK YOU, KOGARASUMARU.
PLEASE KEEP LOOKING OUT FOR ME.

ALL RIGHT.
WELL, THEN...

LET'S GO.

LOG HORIZON
THE WEST WIND BRIGADE

LOG HORIZON
THE WEST WIND BRIGADE

LOG HORIZON
THE WEST WIND BRIGADE

KUROE.

THE EQUIP HUNTER.
WHERE IS HE?

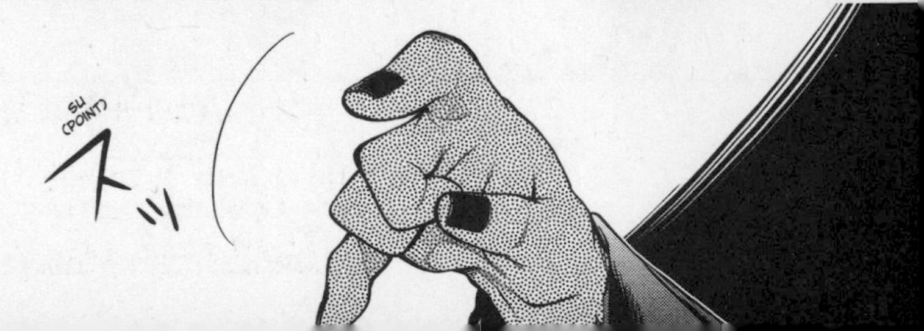
SU (POINT)
スッ

CHAPTER: 56 Third Time

MUD.

MUD,
MUD
...
MUD,
MUD
...

WHO...
...AM
I?

WHO
AM...
...I?

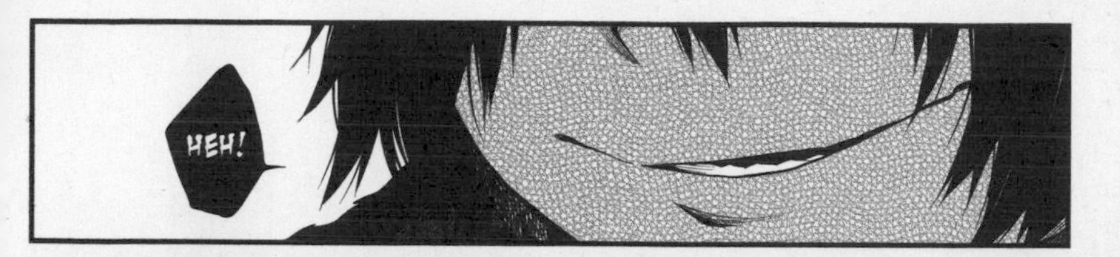
HEH!

U FU FU!
U FU FU FU FU!
AH HA HA HA HA!

THAT DOESN'T MATTER NOW...

THE MUD IS WHERE I BELONG ANYWAY.

MURKY ...
FILTHY ...
WHERE NOBODY CAN SEE.

ADVEN-TURERS.
PEOPLE OF THE EARTH.
MON-STERS.
THIS WORLD.
I'LL DEFILE THEM.
BREAK THEM.
SINK IT ALL INTO THE MUD.
AND THEN, FINALLY...
...WE'LL BE AT ZERO—THE BEGINNING.
IF EVERYONE STARTS FROM DEEP IN THE MUD, THEN IT DOESN'T MATTER WHAT I AM NOW...
... RIGHT?

I AM RIGHT, AREN'T I...
...ME?

SOMEBODY SAID SOMETHING LIKE THIS—
"BY MAKING A PLACE FOR SOMEONE ELSE TO BELONG...
...YOU CREATE A PLACE FOR YOURSELF."

AND SO...
...I'LL PULL EVERYTHING DOWN HERE, INTO THE MUD.

SHIRO-SENPAI SAID THOSE WORDS, BUT THAT'S NOT WHAT HE MEANT.

COME...
...HERE.
!
ZA (SHUF)
ザッ
BAN (WHAP)
GA (GRAB)
ガッ

UNGH!
DADDY ...

KEEP YOUR WITS ABOUT YOU.

NAZUNA.
TAKE CARE OF KUROE.
YESSIR.

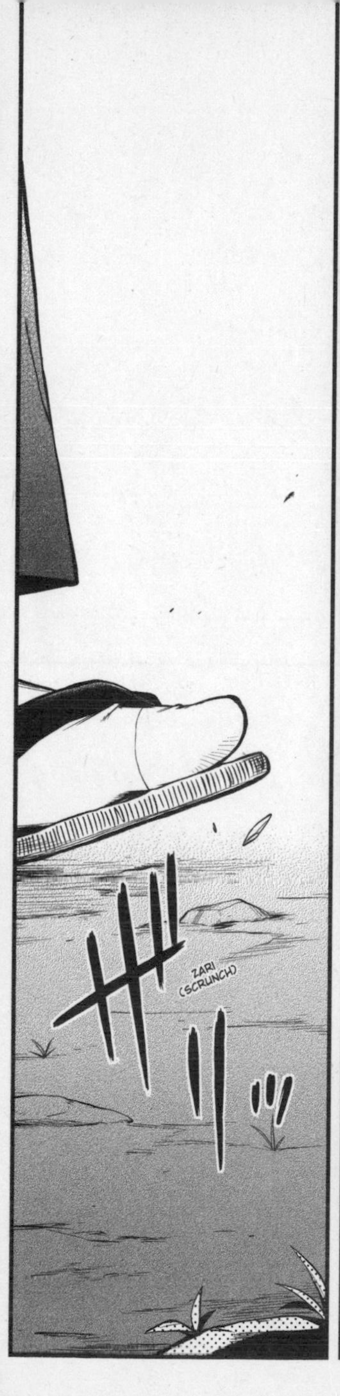
ZARI (SCRUNCH)

KIN (SHING)
ZU (ZZT)
ズ
ZU
ズ...

GIIII (CLAAAANG)
ギ GI
GI ギ
GI ギ
ZU (ZZZT)
I'M GLAD YOU PURPOSELY CAME TO A PLACE OUTSIDE THE CITY, WHERE IT'S EASIER TO FIGHT.
IT'S EASIER...

ZO
ZO
...FOR ME TOO!!
...!!
GI (CLANG)
I CAN CRUSH YOU WITHOUT HOLDING BACK.
SOUJI!!
I'M FINE.
TO (TMP)
DORO (GLORP)

BARA (SPATTER)
IT'S ANNOYING HAVING ANOTHER ME AROUND...!!
DO
DO (THOOM)
YOU'RE WELL-LIKED BY EVERYBODY.
PULSE BULLET!!
NOT ONLY THAT, BUT YOU'RE BETTER OFF THAN I AM.
DO
DO
DO
NOBODY LOOKS DOWN ON YOU!!
DO
DO
DO
DO

ZU (ZZT)
BO (BOOMF)
BO
BO
BO
BO

BA (TURN)
PARA (PATTER)
PARA
NOBODY THINKS YOU AND THE BOSS...
...ARE THE SAME.

...YOU ALL DO.
YOU DENY ME!!
DO (LUNGE)
ISAMI-CHAN, GET BACK!!
ZA (SHUF)
ZA
WHY DO YOU PROTECT HER!?
WHY DO YOU RISK YOUR LIVES!?

SHE'S DIFFERENT FROM YOU!!
GA
GA (CLANK)
GA
THAT'S NOT TRUE!!
GA
GA

SHE'S OUR FRIEND!
NO... WE'VE SPENT ALL OUR TIME IN THIS WORLD TOGETHER, SO...
...SHE'S MORE THAN THAT!!

MERE WORDS.
YOU ONLY MEAN THEM ON THE SURFACE...

OTHER PEOPLE ARE THE ENEMY!!
EVEN IF YOU SPEND TIME TOGETHER.
EVEN IF THEY'RE BLOOD RELA-TIVES.
ALL OF THEM... ALL OF THEM!!

—!! WHAT'S WITH THESE TUBES!?
BYUOO (HWOOO)
THERE ARE...
...WAY TOO MANY!!
DON'T LET THE RECOVERY LAPSE!!
BACHI (KRAKL)
BACHI
WILLOW SPIRITS!! ASTRAL BIND!!
BOKO
BOKO (GRUNK)
BOKO

GISHI (CREAK)
...TCH!
TO (TMP)
GYURU (SPIN)
GYURU
HIYAAAA-AAAAH!!

GA
GA (DAK)
ROUND WINDMILL!!
GA
GA
MAGUS-CHAN! WE'LL ATTACK IN ONE BLOW!!
GYAAAN (BWAAANG)
MAESTRO ECHO!!
GYUIIIN (BWAOOOAA)
BURNED STAKE!!
GOBO (BLORP)
GOBO

GOOOO (FOOOOM)
GAAAAAAAH!!
OOO (OOO)

BO
(BOOMF)
GA
(CLANK)
OH
CRAP—
ZU
ZU
(ZZT)

ISAMI-SAN!!
BACHI (KRAKL)
ELECTRIC FLASH!!
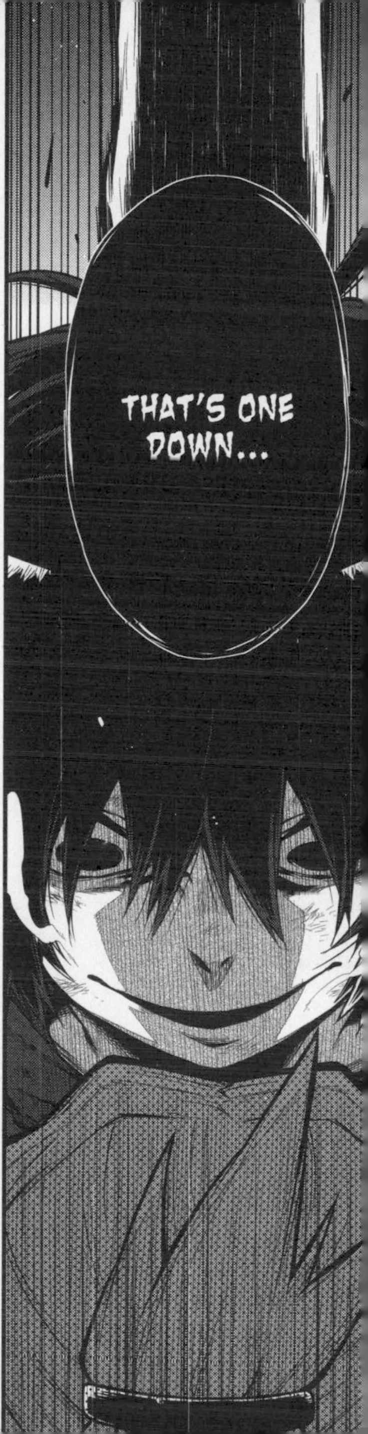
THAT'S ONE DOWN...

WE WON'T LET YOU—!!
GI (CREAK)
OOO (OOO)
DO (SHUNK)
DO
DO
OOO
GYOO (WHROOSH)

DO
(SKASH)

IF MY SPIRIT IS WITHIN YOU, THEN...
...THE PERSON YOU NEED TO PROTECT SHOULD BE KEPT CLOSEST TO YOU.

IF YOU CAN'T DO THAT, MY WEAKNESS MUST BE TO BLAME.
BREAK IT... ALL...
...UNTIL IT'S MUD...
YOUR SINS ARE MY SINS.
AND SO I'LL SHOULDER THOSE SINS.
I'LL CUT THROUGH YOUR NEGATIVE CHAINS.
BO (BOH)
BO
BO

FIRE-
WHEEL
SWORD
!!

GAKU
DOBA (BLOOSH)
GAKU (SHUDDER)
DOSA (FWUMP)

DADDY...

SOUJIROU-KUN, YOU'VE GOTTA DESTROY THE CORE...
I KNOW...

DOKUN
(BADMP)

DOKUN
DOKUN

WHAT'S
...
...THIS
CHILLING
AURA...!?
DOKUN
DOKUN
DOKUN

OOOOO (HWOOO)
GIRO (GLARE)

LOG HORIZON
THE WEST WIND BRIGADE

LOG HORIZON
THE WEST WIND BRIGADE

OOOOO (HWOOO)
DOKUN (BADMP)
DOKUN
DOKUN
LOG HORIZON
THE WEST WIND BRIGADE
SU (RAISE)

BACHI (SNAP)
DO (WHUD)
... HUH?

スゥ…
SUU (RAISE)

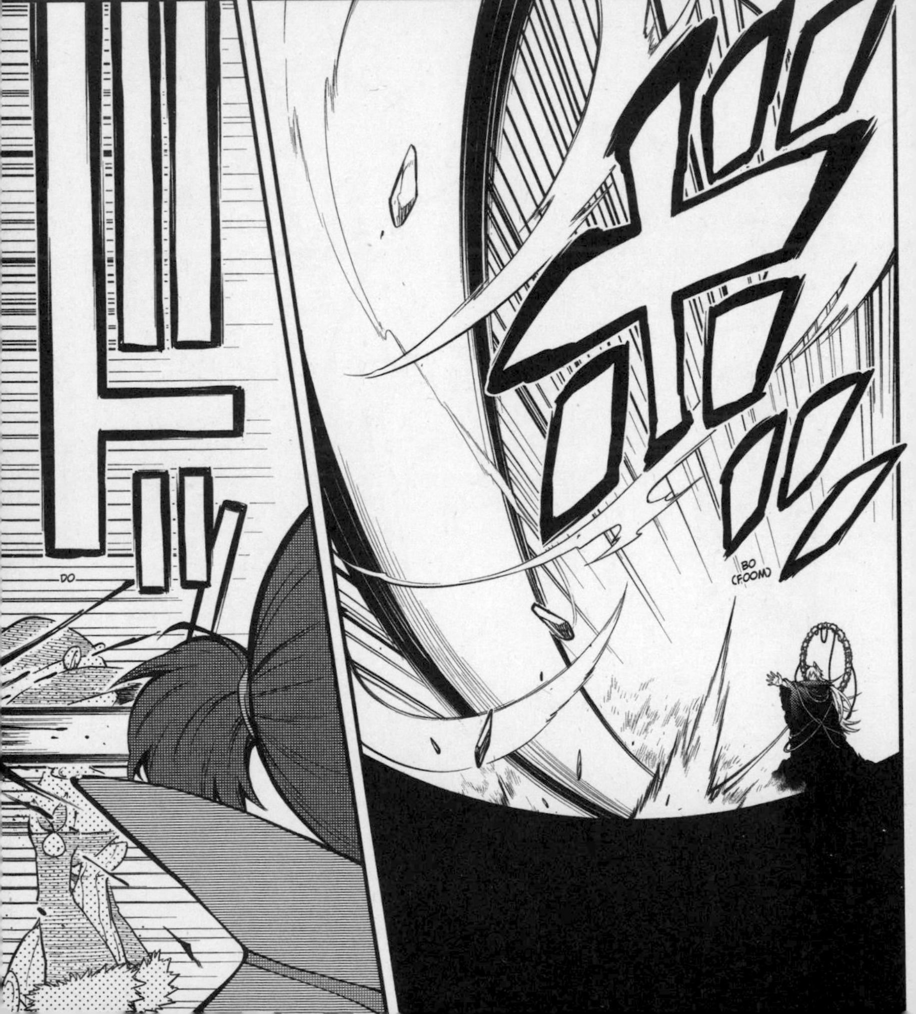
ドッ
DO
ボオオオ
BO (FOOM)

GOFU (BLUCK)
...!!
DOSA (FWUMP)
IN THIS WORLD, EVERYBODY HAS "HP."
I KILLED THEM, HUH? THIS POWER'S HARD TO CONTROL...
0 / 11
HP
7994
MP
HP IS LIFE ENERGY. IF IT RUNS OUT, THAT MEANS YOU'RE DEAD.

HOWEVER, IN THIS WORLD, DEATH ISN'T THE END—NOT FOR ADVENTURERS.
EVEN IF WE GET HURT, COLLAPSE, AND DIE, WE KNOW WE'LL REVIVE IN THE TEMPLE AFTER SOME TIME.

IN OTHER WORDS, EVEN IF OUR HP HITS ZERO, IF SOMEONE CAST A RESURRECTION SPELL PROMPTLY, WE COULD REVIVE ON THE SPOT.
ON TOP OF THAT, FOR THE MEMBERS OF A GUILD ON THE WEST WIND BRIGADE'S LEVEL, DYING IN BATTLE ISN'T UNUSUAL.

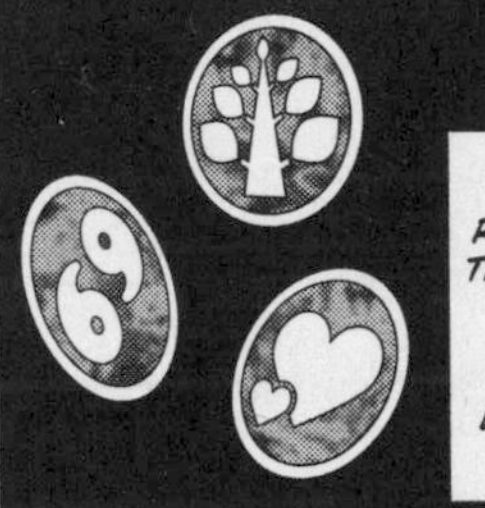
MOST OF ALL, ADVENTURERS IN THE RECOVERY CLASSES...
...LEARN RESURRECTION SPELLS WHILE THEY'RE STILL LOW-LEVEL PLAYERS.

BUT...
...NONE OF US COULD MOVE.

IT IS PRECISELY BECAUSE WE'D FOUGHT AGAINST SO MANY TOUGH ENEMIES TO THE DEATH IN THE GAME THAT...
...IN THAT MOMENT, WE ALL REACHED THE SAME CONCLUSION—

CHAPTER : 57 A Single Arrow

GA (DAK)
ガ
GA
ガ
GA
ガ
GA
ガ
ALL MEMBERS!
RETREAT!!
DO (FOOM)
ジャラ
JYARA (RATTLE)

...!! IT'S NO GOOD, SOUJI!!
WE CAN'T GET AWAY...
THAT'S... ISAAC-SAN'S...!?

NO.
GIRI
GIRI (STRAIN)
HE'S FORCIBLY RESTRICTING OUR RANGE OF MOVEMENT ...
HNRRRRGH!
DID HE BOOST BLACK SWORD OF PAIN'S ABILITIES?
IF THIS KEEPS UP...
...WHAT SHOULD WE DO? THINK!

THINKING WON'T HELP YOU NOW...
ZU (ZZZT)

RGH ...!!
BA (YANK)

CHI (SNIK)
JI (SHIK)
DO (WHUD)
DO
HE'S NOT EVEN TRYING TO BLOCK THE KATANA. OR NO—
HE'S SO STRONG HE DOESN'T NEED TO!!
DO
ZA
ZA (SHUF)
I DON'T KNOW WHAT THE SOURCE OF HIS MANA IS...
DOKUN
DOKUN (BADMP)
...BUT HE'S DEFINITELY DRAWING IT UP FROM THE GROUND.
IN THAT CASE, FOR STARTERS... I'LL CUT THE SUPPLY!!
DA (DASH)

DO
THE BLADE BARELY NICKED IT!
GICHI (SKRIK)
GYURU (FLIP)
SUPPORT ATTACK!!
BA (LUNGE)

GO
(WHUD)

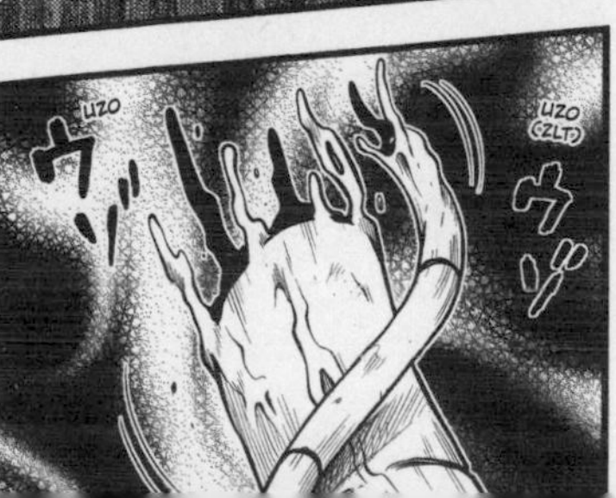
UZO
UZO
(ZLT)

WE CUT IT!!
YEAH!

ZO (ZZT)
GICHI (SKRIK)
SOUJI! GET BACK!!
IT REGEN-ERATES FAST TOO—!!
ZO
ZO
BA (LEAP)

ZU
(ZZUM)

DA (TA)
DAN (TMP)

ELEMENTAL RAY!!
MIRROR'S MYSTIC SPELL!!
ZA (SHUF)

WHAT'S YOUR TAKE ON THIS, NAZUNA!?
IF WE PUT OUR ALL INTO DEFENSE AND RECOVERY...I'D SAY WE'VE GOT TEN MINUTES, MAYBE.

IF WE RUN OUT OF MP...
...HE'LL DEMOLISH US.

UNFORTU-NATELY, I WAS THINKING THE SAME...
MOU (BILLOW)
MOU

FOR NOW, WE GOTTA DO SOMETHING ABOUT *THESE*—
JYARA (CLINK)

DO (WHUD)
—HUH!? WHEN DID HE...!?
BLUGH!
NAZU-NA!!
GO (THUNK)
BAKYA (FOOM)
GA (WHUD)

MMPH !!
GASHI (GRAB)
NAZUNA-TAN! HANG IN THERE!
KOFF!
BLEGH!
AGH!
BACHI (SNAP)
BAH (LUNGE)
TOO SLOW.
TO (TUP)

"IF WE PUT OUR ALL INTO DEFENSE AND RECOVERY..."
...WHAT WAS THAT YOU WERE SAYING?
GISHI (KRIKK)
GISHI
GIRI (GRRR)
GIRI
BOKIN (SNAP)
UGK!
...!!

AH...
AAAH...
SOU... JI...
PAAA (GLOOOW)

DA...

DADDYYYYYYYYYYYY!!
BEKI (KRAKK)
BOKIN

GHK...!!
HE SNAPPED IT LIKE A TWIG!!
DAN (TMP)
HE'S EVEN STRONGER THAN I IMAGINED!!
WHY, YOU ...!!
I'LL BACK YOU UP!!
RECOVERY!!
SOU-SAMA!!
BA (SWING)
!!

IT'S NO USE...

OUR RECOVERY CAN'T KEEP UP!

THINK ...
THERE MUST BE SOME WAY TO ESCAPE THIS SITUATION...

IT'S A HARD PROCESS TO MAKE THOSE, AND WE COULD ONLY GET ONE READY.
YOU BETTER NOT MISS.
...I KNOW.

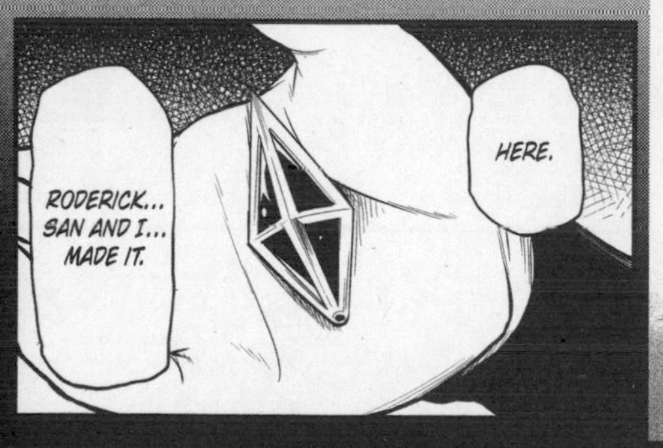
HERE.
RODERICK... SAN AND I... MADE IT.

WHAT IS IT? AN ARROW-HEAD?
THIS CONTAINS THE BLOOD OF SEVERAL ADVENTUR-ERS.
THE EQUIP HUNTER AVOIDS ATTACKING ADVENTURERS DIRECTLY BECAUSE HE CAN'T SELECTIVELY ABSORB OR DISCARD INFORMATION.
HE'S PROBABLY THINKING ABOUT THE POSSIBILITY OF ABSORBING BLOOD FROM HIS VICTIMS.
IF WE FORCE HIM TO TAKE IN A LOT OF INFORMATION, HE MAY LOSE CONTROL AND SELF-DESTRUCT.

WHAT IF HE JUST GETS STRONGER...?
THAT COULD HAPPEN TOO, OF COURSE...

AND SO, CONSIDER IT FOR EMERGENCIES ONLY...

SOMETHING TO USE IN A MOMENT OF DESPERATION.

TO THINK WE'D ACTUALLY END UP USING IT...
......

PLEASE ...!
SAVE EVERYONE—
SAVE THE BOSS!
GU (PULL)
GU

AND WHAT...
...HAVE YOU BEEN PLOTTING IN WHISPERS OVER THERE, HM?
GYUOOO (WHROOSH)
OOO (OOO)
KYUN (VREEN)

GYUOOO
ROOK SLIDER!!
AAAAAAA-
AAAAAAH!!

TO
(THUNK)

LOG HORIZON
THE WEST WIND BRIGADE

LOG HORIZON
THE WEST WIND BRIGADE

LOG HORIZON
THE WEST WIND BRIGADE
THIS CONTAINS THE BLOOD OF SEVERAL ADVENTURERS.
PLEASE ...!!
SAVE EVERYONE—
AAAAAAAA
AAAAAAH!!

CHAPTER : 58 No Good

SAVE THE BOSS!!

DO <THUNK>

IF WE FORCE HIM TO TAKE IN A LOT OF INFORMATION...
...HE MAY LOSE CONTROL AND SELF-DESTRUCT.
...IS IT DOING ANY-THING!?
PLEASE ...!!
ZA (SHF)
ZA

PLEASE LET THIS WORK!!

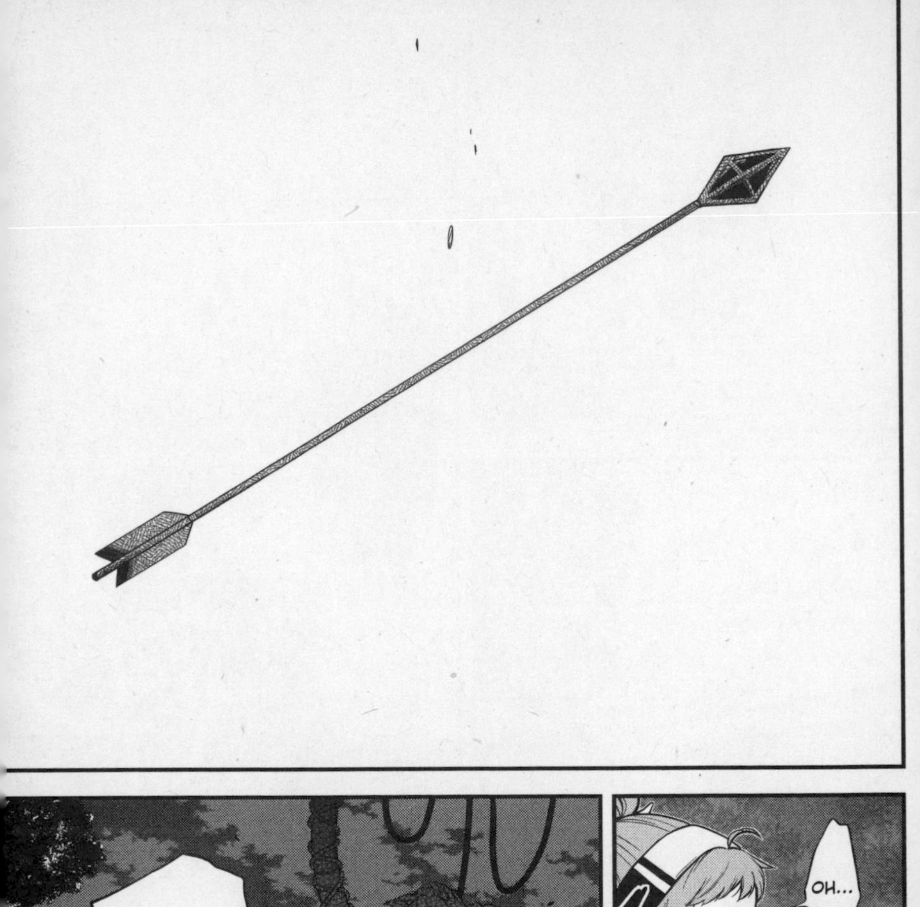

OH...
N...
NO...
KARAN
(CLANG)
IT DIDN'T
EVEN...PIERCE
HIM...!

YOU TWO—
WEREN'T YOU EVEN WATCHING ...?
EARLIER, YOUR BELOVED SOUJIROU SWUNG HIS SWORD AT ME, OVER AND OVER...
...AND IT BARELY EVEN LEFT A SCRATCH.
DID YOU REALLY THINK...
...A LITTLE THING LIKE THIS COULD BRING ME DOWN?

THE BLOOD OF ADVEN-TURERS, HM...?
ZA (SHF)
I SEE...
ZA
SO THIS WAS YOUR TRUMP CARD.
ZA
ZA
...!

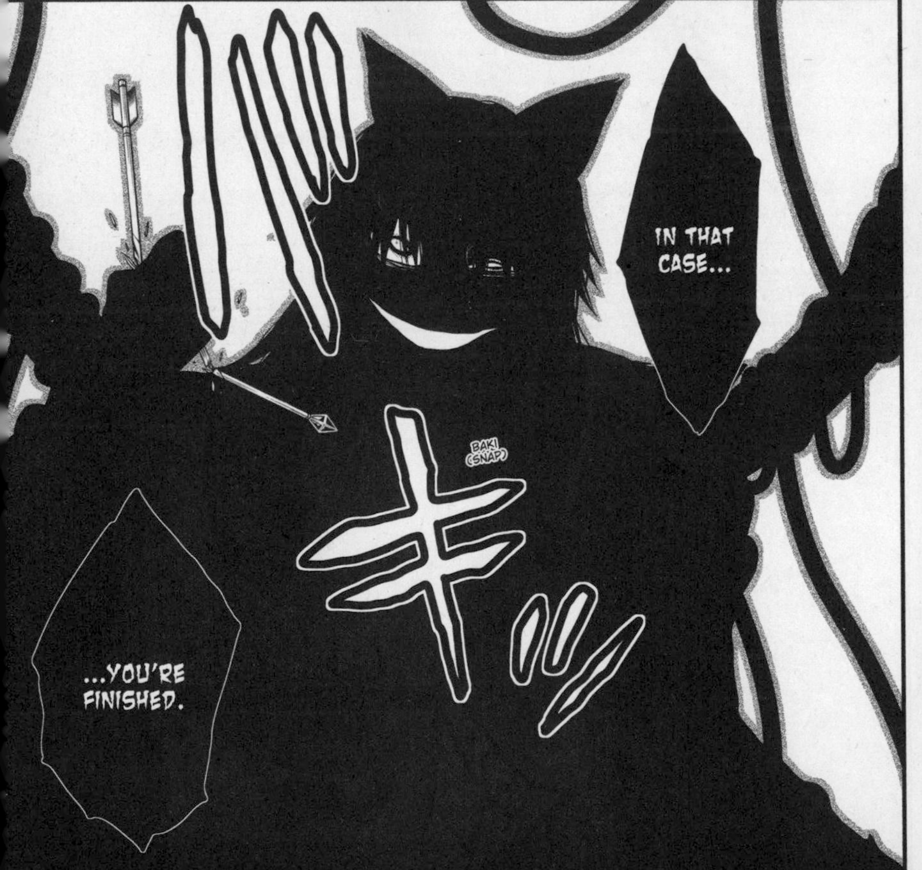
IN THAT CASE...
BAKI (SNAP)
...YOU'RE FINISHED.

BAKI (KRAK)
GA (WHACK)
GO (THUD)
BISHA (SPLAT)
PA (PLIP)
PA

BOTA (DRIP)
BOTA
NOT YET...
YOU CAN'T DIE YET.

I KILLED THOSE FIRST TWO BY ACCIDENT...
...BUT I'VE GOTTEN THE HANG OF CONTROLLING MY STRENGTH NOW.
グ
GU (STRAIN)
ゴホッ
GOHO (KOFF)
グ
GU
グ
GU
グ
GU
TAKE A GOOD LOOK.
SEE HOW MESSED UP THEY ARE?
THAT'S ALL YOUR FAULT.

NOW, THEN...
GUN (FOOM)
GO (WHUD)
BYUO (WHOOSH)
GHAK!!

HYUU (WHEEZE)
HYUU
......
ALL RIGHT, ME.
YOU'VE GOT A GREAT SEAT THERE. WATCH CLOSELY...

ZU
(ZZT)
AS
I...
...EAT
HER.
ZU
ZU
ZU
AH...
NO...

GU (TUG)
ZU (ZZT)
HFF!
HFF!
.....!
DO (SHUNK)
...!!

BUSHI (SLISH)
AGH!
GHK...!!

LET GO.

DO
DOSU (SHUNK)
AUGH!
AH!
DOSU
DOSU
AAH ...!!
GAH!
DOSU
DOSU
YEAAAAAAUGH!!
DOSU

NO MORE...

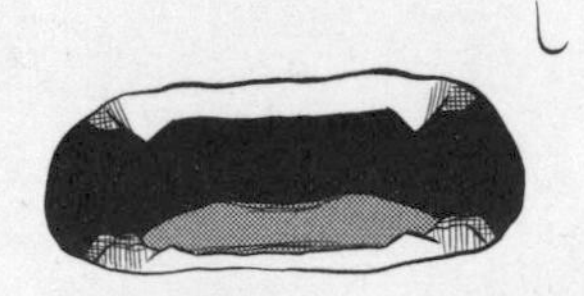

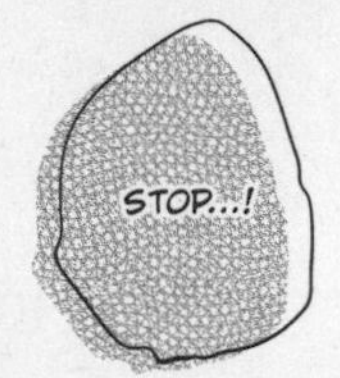
STOP...!

PLEASE! STOP HURTING DADDY!!
NO...
I'LL... GO BACK TO YOU...
...SO DON'T BE MEAN TO DADDY ANYMORE...

YOU CAN'T ...
...DO THAT.
DADDY... THANK YOU...
I'M SORRY FOR CAUSING YOU TROUBLE.
IT'S OKAY. I'M JUST GOING BACK TO WHAT I USED TO BE...
BACK TO SOMETHING... THAT'S NOT A PERSON...
IT WASN'T FOR VERY LONG, BUT, DADDY...
...I WAS HAPPY I GOT TO BE WITH YOU AND THE GUILD.

BIKU (FLINCH)
I TOLD YOU...
...YOU CAN'T DO THAT!!

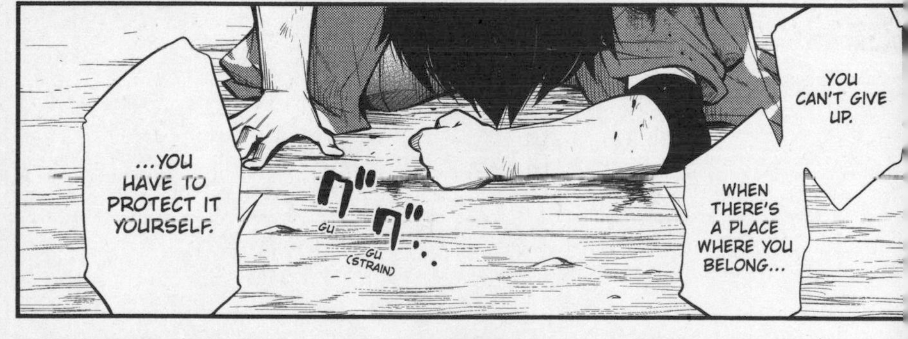
YOU CAN'T GIVE UP.
WHEN THERE'S A PLACE WHERE YOU BELONG...
GU GU (STRAIN)
...YOU HAVE TO PROTECT IT YOURSELF.

DADDY...
I DON'T KNOW WHERE YOU'RE GETTING THESE IDEAS, BUT...

...THE PLACE SHE AND I BELONG IS DEEP IN THE MUD.
WE DON'T MIX WITH OTHERS...
DON'T LUMP KUROE IN WITH YOU.
YORO (STAGGER)
KUROE IS KUROE—
SHE'S NOT YOU!!
...! SHUT UP...
SHUT YOUR MOUTH.

EVEN IF THAT WERE TRUE ...
...IT HAS NOTHING TO DO WITH YOU!!
BYU (WHIRR)
GHK!!
GIRI (CLENCH)
YES ...
...IT DOES!
KUROE, LISTEN—
IF YOU WANT TO...
...YOU CAN STAY WITH US FOREVER.

WE ONCE HAD AN EARNEST BATTLE.
YOU WERE KIND ENOUGH TO NEED ME.
AND...

...YOU STAYED WITH ME.

WHEN IT COMES TO YOU, KUROE...

...AND THE PEOPLE WHO STAY BY MY SIDE...
...AND THE PLACE I BELONG—

I'LL PROTECT ALL OF IT!

ALL RIGHT ...
THAT'S ENOUGH.

I THOUGHT I'D KIL YOUR FRIENDS ONE BY ONE, BURY YOU DEEP IN DESPAIR...
...THEN KILL YOU LAST OF ALL, BUT ENOUGH! THIS IS IRRITATING!!
BOH (BOOMF)
THE FIRST ONE TO DIE WILL BE—

BESHA (FLUMP)
...!
KU... RO...?
KUROE...
...KUROE!

AAAAAAAAAAHHHH

LOG HORIZON
THE WEST WIND BRIGADE

LOG HORIZON
THE WEST WIND BRIGADE

LOG HORIZON
THE WEST WIND BRIGADE
I LIKED FIGHTING.

I WATCHED ANIME...
...AND READ MANGA...

...AND WHEN THE HEROES FOUGHT THE BAD GUYS, I WANTED TO BE THEM.

BEFORE I KNEW IT...
...I STARTED PLAYING ELDER TALES.

EVEN IF IT WAS IMAGINARY, IN THAT WORLD, I COULD FIGHT LIKE THE HEROES I IDOLIZED.
IT STOLE MY HEART IN AN INSTANT, AND I WAS HOOKED.
AND THEN...

...I MET PEOPLE I COULD RESPECT...
...AND FOUND A NEW PLACE TO BELONG.

THEY WEREN'T THE SORT OF PEOPLE WHO CHOSE THEIR COMPANIONS...
...BASED ON WHETHER THEY WERE USEFUL OR NOT OR WHETHER THERE WAS ANYTHING IN IT FOR THEM.

EVEN SO...
...I REALLY ENJOYED THE TIME I SPENT WITH THEM...
...AND WANTED TO MAKE MYSELF USEFUL.

I WASN'T ALL THAT BRIGHT...

...SO...

...I THOUGHT I'D WORK HARDER AND HARDER...
...AT THE FIGHTING I LOVED SO MUCH.

BEFORE I EVEN REALIZED...
...I'D BECOME A RELATIVELY FAMOUS PLAYER.

THAT DIDN'T MEAN I GOT OVERCONFIDENT IN MY OWN STRENGTH.
I DIDN'T, BUT...
...I WAS STRONG ENOUGH TO PROTECT THE PEOPLE WHO WERE IMPORTANT TO ME.
AT LEAST...
...THAT'S WHAT I THOUGHT.

I THOUGHT SO...

...EVEN AFTER THE CATASTROPHE.

GISHI (CREAK)
BUT WHEN IT CAME DOWN TO IT, WHAT HAPPENED?
I DIDN'T PROTECT THEM. IN FACT, I PUT THEM IN DANGER.

I LOST FIGHTS...
ZUAAA (FWIIIISH)
...AND THEY ENDED UP SAVING ME INSTEAD.

AND...
...NOW...

...I DON'T HAVE THE STRENGTH TO PROTECT HER.

AAAAAAAAAA
WH... WHY...?

...ROE.
KUROE!

KUROE...

I-IT'S... O...
...KAY...

I'M LIKE HIM...
UNLESS THE CORE BREAKS, I'LL BE...FINE...
DOKUN (BADMP)
DOKUN

THAT'S NOT THE PROBLEM!!
WHY...?
YEAH...
WHY!?

WHY WOULD WE...
...PRO-TECT SOME-ONE!?

THAT'S NOT...
THAT'S NOT... RIGHT!
I—!
I—! I! AH! AAAH!
AAAAA

DADDY...
GEHO (KOFF)
GOHO (KOFF)
DON'T TALK!!
IT'S OKAY. YOU DON'T HAVE TO TALK RIGHT NOW.
I'LL...
I'LL TAKE YOU SOME-WHERE SAFE...
DADDY... LISTEN...

I'LL PROTECT...
...EVERY-BODY...

...AND...
...I WILL...
...END HIM.

GIVE HER...
...TO ME!!
ZO (ZZT)
SHE'S NOT A PART OF ME ANYMORE!!
I DON'T HAVE THAT...!
I DON'T NEED IT!!

I'LL WIPE YOU OUT OF EXISTENCE! DISAPPEAR!
VANISH!
VANISH!
VANIIIISH!!

MAKE EVERY-THING GO AWAY!!
GO
(THOOM)

GO
GO

BOGO (GRUNCH)
BAGA (BLAM)
BAKI (KRAK)
BAKI
AAAAAAAAAAAA
BEKI (SNAP)
BEKI
ZU
ZUUUUUN (BOOOOOM)
GA (DAK)
GA
GA
GA

BEKI
BAKI

HFF!
HFF!

I...
ME...?
PRO... TECT...?
EVERY-THING... ALL OF IT... DEEP IN THE MUD...
DEFEAT...
CRUSH.
ERASE.
DEGRADE...

WHY ...?
DO (THOOM)
HOW ARE YOU STILL STANDING !?
DO
DO
DO

DO
DO
DO
DO
DO
DO
DO
DO
OOOO (OOOO)
MY ATTACKS AREN'T HITTING THEM...!?
WHY...
WHY!?
HFF
HFF

GYU
(SQUEEZE)

DADDY, LISTEN—
YOU ARE STRONG.

IT WAS JUST FOR A LITTLE WHILE...
...BUT I WATCHED YOU AND SAW...YOU WORKED REALLY, REALLY HARD.

EVERY-BODY KNOWS YOU'RE STRONG.
SOU... JI...
THE ONLY ONE WHO DOESN'T KNOW...

...IS YOU, DADDY.

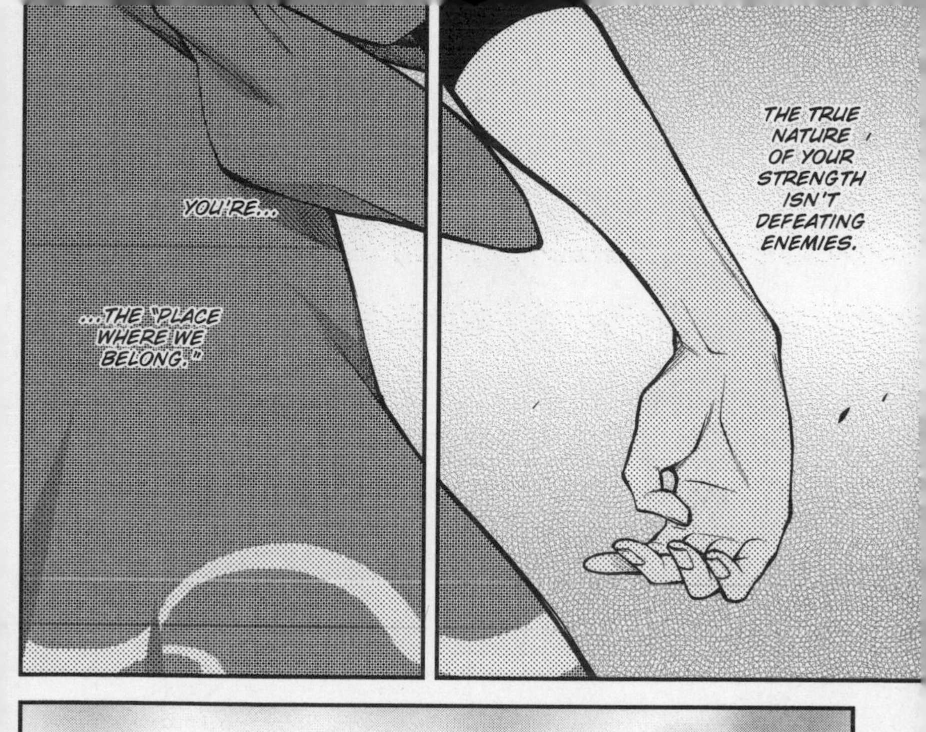

THE TRUE NATURE OF YOUR STRENGTH ISN'T DEFEATING ENEMIES.
YOU'RE...
...THE "PLACE WHERE WE BELONG."

BECAUSE YOU'RE HERE...
...WE CAN ALL FACE OUR FOES.
BECAUSE YOU'RE HERE...
...WE CAN KEEP SMILING.
BECAUSE YOU'RE HERE...
...WE CAN GET UP AGAIN AND AGAIN.

YOU DON'T WANT...
...ANY OF US TO GET HURT, SO...
...YOU DON'T HESITATE TO STEP OUT IN FRONT...
...AND TAKE THAT DAMAGE YOURSELF.

BUT IT'S NOT RIGHT.
THAT'S NOT HOW IT SHOULD BE.
YOU...
...HAVE TO STAY STANDING UNTIL THE VERY END.
THAT'S WHAT GIVES...
...THE REST OF US STRENGTH.
IT'S ALL RIGHT.
YOU'RE STRONG, DADDY.
YOU JUST HAVEN'T NOTICED YOUR POWER YET, THAT'S ALL—

I'LL...

...TEACH YOU HOW TO USE THAT STRENGTH.

MYSTERY

CLAIR-VOYANCE.

To be continued in Volume 11

Special Thanks
AOKI-SAN
SAASHI-SAN
ITSUKA-SAN

LOG HORIZON
THE WEST WIND BRIGADE ⑩

Art: Koyuki
Original Story: Mamare Touno
Character Design: Kazuhiro Hara

Translation: Taylor Engel
Lettering: Brndn Blakeslee

This book is a work of fiction. Names, characters, places, and incidents are the product of the author's imagination or are used fictitiously. Any resemblance to actual events, locales, or persons, living or dead, is coincidental.

LOG HORIZON NISHIKAZE NO RYODAN volume 10
© KOYUKI 2017
© TOUNO MAMARE, KAZUHIRO HARA 2017
First published in Japan in 2017 by KADOKAWA CORPORATION, Tokyo.
English translation rights arranged with KADOKAWA CORPORATION, Tokyo, through Tuttle-Mori Agency, Inc., Tokyo.

English translation © 2018 by Yen Press, LLC

Yen Press, LLC supports the right to free expression and the value of copyright. The purpose of copyright is to encourage writers and artists to produce the creative works that enrich our culture.

The scanning, uploading, and distribution of this book without permission is a theft of the author's intellectual property. If you would like permission to use material from the book (other than for review purposes), please contact the publisher. Thank you for your support of the author's rights.

Yen Press
1290 Avenue of the Americas
New York, NY 10104

Visit us at yenpress.com
facebook.com/yenpress
twitter.com/yenpress
yenpress.tumblr.com
instagram.com/yenpress

First Yen Press Edition: November 2018

Yen Press is an imprint of Yen Press, LLC.
The Yen Press name and logo are trademarks of Yen Press, LLC.

The publisher is not responsible for websites (or their content) that are not owned by the publisher.

Library of Congress Control Number: 2015952586

ISBN: 978-1-9753-2811-5 (paperback)

10 9 8 7 6 5 4 3 2 1

WOR

Printed in the United States of America